TRIVIA
FOR
GENIUS MINDS

Table of Contents

- **150 Trivial Facts**

- **150 Quizzes * True or False ***

- **150 Fun Questions**

What's Inside

⟹ **"450 Mind-Blowing Facts for Genius Minds"** covers a wide range of topics, from biology and astronomy to physics and history, offering informative and entertaining knowledge. You'll be amazed by the intriguing facts about planets and stars, your curiosity will be piqued by the facts about animals and plants, and your knowledge will be enriched by the incredible historical and geographical facts. The book adds a fun element with multiple-choice quizzes that test your knowledge and stimulate your thinking.

<u>FACTS</u>

** Enrich your Knowledge **

1. The human brain weighs about 3 pounds but uses 20% of the body's energy.

2. The Eiffel Tower can be 15 cm taller during hot days due to thermal expansion.

3. Octopuses have three hearts and blue blood.

4. The shortest war in history lasted 38 minutes between Britain and Zanzibar in 1896.

5. The average person walks the equivalent of three times around the world in a lifetime.

6. Bananas are berries, but strawberries aren't.

7. There are more stars in the universe than grains of sand on Earth.

8. Honey never spoils; archaeologists have found pots of honey in ancient Egyptian tombs that are over 3,000 years old and still edible.

9. The human nose can detect about one trillion different scents.

10. A day on Venus is longer than a year on Venus.

11. Sharks have been around longer than trees.

12. The world's smallest reptile was discovered in 2021—a tiny chameleon that can fit on a fingertip.

13. The total weight of ants on Earth is roughly equal to the weight of all humans.

14. There are more possible iterations of a game of chess than there are atoms in the known universe.

15. The smell of fresh-cut grass is actually a plant distress call.

16. Light from the Sun takes about 8 minutes and 20 seconds to reach Earth.

17. If you could fold a piece of paper 42 times, it would reach the moon.

18. A cloud can weigh more than a million pounds.

19. There's a species of jellyfish that is immortal—it can revert to its juvenile form after reaching adulthood.

20. Cows have best friends and can become stressed when separated.

21. Venus is the hottest planet in our solar system, despite not being the closest to the Sun.

22. More people live in Tokyo than in Canada.

23. Bees can recognize human faces.

24. The longest hiccuping spree lasted 68 years.

25. An octopus has nine brains—one central brain and one in each of its eight arms.

26. Jupiter's Great Red Spot is a storm that has been raging for at least 400 years.

27. A bolt of lightning contains enough energy to toast 100,000 slices of bread.

28. The fingerprints of koalas are almost indistinguishable from humans.

29. Humans share 60% of their DNA with bananas.

30. The moon is slowly moving away from Earth at a rate of about 1.5 inches per year.

31. Sloths can hold their breath longer than dolphins.

32. Cleopatra lived closer in time to the first Moon landing than to the construction of the Great Pyramid of Giza.

33. The human stomach gets a new lining every three to four days to prevent it from digesting itself.

34. The longest recorded flight of a chicken is 13 seconds.

35. A group of flamingos is called a "flamboyance."

36. A single strand of spaghetti is called a "spaghetto."

37. Hot water freezes faster than cold water, a phenomenon known as the Mpemba effect.

38. There are more trees on Earth than stars in the Milky Way galaxy.

39. If Betelgeuse, a red supergiant star, were placed at the center of our solar system, its outer layers would extend beyond the orbit of Jupiter.

40. Dolphins have names for each other and can call out to specific individuals.

41. There's a planet made of diamond twice the size of Earth.

42. Butterflies taste with their feet.

43. Some metals are so reactive that they explode on contact with water.

44. Wombat poop is cube-shaped.

45. The Eiffel Tower can sway up to 7 inches in the wind.

46. Your body has more bacterial cells than human cells.

47. Sea otters hold hands while sleeping to avoid drifting apart.

48. There are more synapses (neural connections) in your brain than there are stars in the Milky Way.

49. Astronauts grow taller in space due to the lack of gravity compressing their spine.

50. Apples float in water because they are 25% air.

51. The largest snowflake ever recorded was 15 inches wide.

52. A snail can sleep for three years.

53. The longest word in the English language is 189,819 letters long.

54. The coldest temperature ever recorded on Earth was -128.6°F in Antarctica.

55. Giraffes have the same number of neck vertebrae as humans—just seven.

56. The Empire State Building has its own zip code.

57. Octopuses have copper-based blood, which makes it blue.

58. In 30 minutes, the human body gives off enough heat to boil a gallon of water.

59. There's a lake in Australia that's naturally bright pink.

60. The shortest complete sentence in the English language is "Go."

61. A blue whale's heart is the size of a small car.

62. The world's oldest piece of chewing gum is over 9,000 years old.

63. A full head of human hair is strong enough to support 12 tons.

64. If you shouted for 8 years, 7 months, and 6 days, you would produce enough sound energy to heat one cup of coffee.

65. You can't hum while holding your nose closed.

66. The average human body contains enough iron to make a 3-inch nail.

67. A flea can accelerate faster than the Space Shuttle.

68. Sharks are the only fish that can blink with both eyes.

69. The Earth's core is as hot as the surface of the Sun.

70. The strongest muscle in the human body is the tongue.

71. A day on Mercury lasts 176 Earth days.

72. Horses and cows sleep while standing up.

73. In Switzerland, it's illegal to own just one guinea pig.

74. An ostrich's eye is bigger than its brain.

75. The average American consumes 35 tons of food in a lifetime.

76. Some fish can recognize their owner's face.

77. It rains diamonds on Saturn and Jupiter.

78. Ants never sleep.

79. A "jiffy" is a real unit of time: 1/100th of a second.

80. The longest recorded wedding veil was longer than 63 football fields.

81. The inventor of the frisbee was turned into a frisbee after he died.

82. Cows can walk upstairs, but not down.

83. A bolt of lightning is five times hotter than the surface of the Sun.

84. The smell of chocolate triggers relaxation in the brain.

85. You can fit all of the planets in our solar system between the Earth and the Moon.

86. The Guinness World Record for the longest hiccuping spree is 68 years.

87. The moon has moonquakes.

88. Bees sometimes sting other bees.

89. Humans are the only animals that blush.

90. The word "set" has the most definitions in the English language.

91. A cloud can weigh more than a million pounds.

92. A group of crows is called a "murder."

93. The word "bookkeeper" has three consecutive double letters.

94. There's a species of spider that keeps frogs as pets.

95. The unicorn is the national animal of Scotland.

96. Cleopatra was born closer in time to the first Moon landing than to the construction of the Great Pyramid.

97. The inventor of the microwave appliance received only $2 for his discovery.

98. A group of porcupines is called a "prickle."

99. Only 5% of the ocean has been explored.

100. A jiffy is an actual unit of time: 1/100th of a second.

101. The tongue of a blue whale weighs more than an elephant.

102. The average person produces enough saliva in their lifetime to fill two swimming pools.

103. The sentence "The quick brown fox jumps over a lazy dog" uses every letter of the alphabet.

104. A hummingbird's heart beats over 1,200 times per minute.

105. Humans are the only animals that enjoy spicy food.

106. There's a species of ant that can make itself explode when threatened.

107. Sea cucumbers can eject their internal organs to scare off predators.

108. Some turtles can breathe through their butts.

109. The Eiffel Tower can grow by up to 6 inches in summer.

110. Octopuses have been observed using tools, a sign of high intelligence.

111. A human could swim through a blue whale's veins.

112. The Earth is not a perfect sphere; it's slightly pear-shaped.**
113. A banana is a berry, but astrawberry isn't.

114. Humans have about the same number of hair follicles as chimpanzees.

115. The oceans contain nearly 200,000 different viruses.

116. Goldfish can see infrared and ultraviolet light.

117. One strand of human hair can support 100 grams of weight.

118. The average person's skin weighs twice as much as their brain.

119. You can boil water at room temperature by lowering the air pressure.

120. The first email was sent by Ray Tomlinson to himself in 1971.

121. The Sahara Desert used to be a lush, green landscape.

122. A group of owls is called a "parliament."

123. The planet Uranus rotates on its side.

124. A bolt of lightning contains enough energy to power a home for a day.

125. The ancient Romans used urine to clean their clothes.

126. Sharks are older than trees.

127. Humans and giraffes have the same number of neck bones.

128. A sneeze can travel up to 100 miles per hour.

129. Hawaii moves closer to Alaska by about 7.5 centimeters every year.

130. Some lizards can detach their tails to escape predators.

131. Butterflies can taste with their feet.

132. A group of rabbits is called a "fluffle."

133. A day on Venus is longer than a year on Venus.

134. An octopus has three hearts.

135. Elephants are the only animals that can't jump.

136. A cat's nose print is unique, much like a human fingerprint.

137. The word "dreamt" is the only word in the English language that ends with "mt."

138. It's impossible to hum while holding your nose.

139. The shortest war in history lasted just 38 minutes.

140. Wombat poop is cube-shaped.

141. The surface area of Russia is larger than the surface area of Pluto.

142. Your stomach gets a new lining every three to four days.

143. A bolt of lightning is five times hotter than the surface of the Sun.

144. The longest English word is 189,819 letters long.

145. Cleopatra lived closer to the Moon landing than to the construction of the Great Pyramid.

146. Sharks can live for five centuries.

147. The average person will walk the equivalent of five times around the Earth in their lifetime.

148. There are more possible iterations of a game of chess than there are atoms in the universe.

149. An octopus has nine brains and three hearts.

150. The only letter that doesn't appear in any U.S. state name is "Q."

QUIEZES

** Choose One of the Correct Answers**

1. **What is the smallest prime number?**
   - A) 0
   - B) 1
   - C) 2
   - D) 3

2. **Who wrote the play "Hamlet"?**
   - A) Charles Dickens
   - B) William Shakespeare
   - C) Mark Twain
   - D) Jane Austen

3. **What is the capital of Australia?**
   - A) Sydney
   - B) Melbourne
   - C) Canberra
   - D) Brisbane

4. **Which element has the chemical symbol 'O'?**
   - A) Gold
   - B) Oxygen
   - C) Osmium
   - D) Mercury

5. **What is the largest planet in our Solar System?**
   - A) Earth
   - B) Mars
   - C) Jupiter
   - D) Saturn

6. **Who painted the Mona Lisa?**
   - A) Vincent van Gogh
   - B) Pablo Picasso
   - C) Leonardo da Vinci
   - D) Claude Monet

7. **Which country is known as the Land of the Rising Sun?**
   - A) China
   - B) Japan
   - C) South Korea
   - D) Thailand

8. **What is the hardest natural substance on Earth?**
   - A) Steel
   - B) Diamond
   - C) Iron
   - D) Quartz

9. **In which year did the Titanic sink?**
   - A) 1905
   - B) 1912
   - C) 1915
   - D) 1920

10. **Who is the author of "1984"?**
    - A) Aldous Huxley
    - B) George Orwell
    - C) J.K. Rowling
    - D) Ernest Hemingway

11. **What is the chemical symbol for gold?**
    - A) Au
    - B) Ag
    - C) Pb
    - D) Fe

12. **Which planet is known as the Red Planet?**
    - A) Venus
    - B) Mars
    - C) Jupiter
    - D) Saturn

13. **Who discovered penicillin?**
    - A) Marie Curie
    - B) Alexander Fleming
    - C) Louis Pasteur
    - D) Isaac Newton

14. **What is the longest river in the world?**
    - A) Nile
    - B) Amazon
    - C) Yangtze
    - D) Mississippi

15. **Which artist cut off his own ear?**
    - A) Leonardo da Vinci
    - B) Michelangelo
    - C) Vincent van Gogh
    - D) Rembrandt

16. **What is the capital of Canada?**
    - A) Toronto
    - B) Vancouver
    - C) Ottawa
    - D) Montreal

17. **What is the largest mammal?**
    - A) Elephant
    - B) Blue Whale
    - C) Hippopotamus

- D) Giraffe

18. **What is the square root of 81?**
    - A) 7
    - B) 8
    - C) 9
    - D) 10

19. **Who is the Greek god of the sea?**
    - A) Zeus
    - B) Hades
    - C) Poseidon
    - D) Apollo

20. **Which element is a noble gas?**
    - A) Hydrogen
    - B) Oxygen
    - C) Neon
    - D) Nitrogen

21. **What is the main ingredient in guacamole?**
    - A) Tomato
    - B) Avocado
    - C) Onion
    - D) Lime

22. **Who wrote "Pride and Prejudice"?**
    - A) Emily Brontë
    - B) Jane Austen
    - C) Charles Dickens
    - D) George Eliot

23. **What is the capital of Egypt?**
    - A) Alexandria
    - B) Giza

  - C) Cairo
  - D) Luxor

24. **Which gas do plants primarily absorb?**
  - A) Oxygen
  - B) Nitrogen
  - C) Carbon Dioxide
  - D) Helium

25. **What is the tallest mountain in the world?**
  - A) K2
  - B) Kangchenjunga
  - C) Mount Everest
  - D) Lhotse

26. **Who is known as the Father of Computers?**
  - A) Alan Turing
  - B) Charles Babbage
  - C) Bill Gates
  - D) Steve Jobs

27. **What is the freezing point of water in Celsius?**
  - A) 0 degrees
  - B) 32 degrees
  - C) 100 degrees
  - D) -1 degree

28. **Which country is home to the kangaroo?**
  - A) India
  - B) Australia
  - C) South Africa
  - D) Brazil

29. **Who painted "The Starry Night"?**
  - A) Edvard Munch

- B) Vincent van Gogh
- C) Claude Monet
- D) Pablo Picasso

30. **What is the boiling point of water in Celsius?**
    - A) 50 degrees
    - B) 100 degrees
    - C) 150 degrees
    - D) 200 degrees

31. **What is the largest ocean on Earth?**
    - A) Atlantic Ocean
    - B) Indian Ocean
    - C) Arctic Ocean
    - D) Pacific Ocean

32. **Who developed the theory of relativity?**
    - A) Nikola Tesla
    - B) Albert Einstein
    - C) Isaac Newton
    - D) Galileo Galilei

33. **Which city is known as the Big Apple?**
    - A) Los Angeles
    - B) New York City
    - C) Chicago
    - D) San Francisco

34. **What is the process by which plants make their food?**
    - A) Respiration
    - B) Digestion
    - C) Photosynthesis
    - D) Fermentation

35. **Who is the author of "The Great Gatsby"?**

- A) Ernest Hemingway
- B) F. Scott Fitzgerald
- C) John Steinbeck
- D) Mark Twain

36. **What is the most abundant gas in Earth's atmosphere?**
    - A) Oxygen
    - B) Nitrogen
    - C) Carbon Dioxide
    - D) Argon

37. **Which planet is closest to the sun?**
    - A) Venus
    - B) Earth
    - C) Mercury
    - D) Mars

38. **Who invented the telephone?**
    - A) Nikola Tesla
    - B) Thomas Edison
    - C) Alexander Graham Bell
    - D) Guglielmo Marconi

39. **What is the largest continent by area?**
    - A) Africa
    - B) Asia
    - C) Europe
    - D) Antarctica

40. **What is the main language spoken in Brazil?**
    - A) Spanish
    - B) English
    - C) Portuguese
    - D) French

41. **Which metal is liquid at room temperature?**
    - A) Iron
    - B) Mercury
    - C) Lead
    - D) Copper

42. **What is the capital of Italy?**
    - A) Venice
    - B) Milan
    - C) Rome
    - D) Florence

43. **Who wrote "The Odyssey"?**
    - A) Homer
    - B) Virgil
    - C) Sophocles
    - D) Euripides

44. **Which planet has the most moons?**
    - A) Earth
    - B) Jupiter
    - C) Saturn
    - D) Mars

45. **What is the primary component of the sun?**
    - A) Oxygen
    - B) Hydrogen
    - C) Nitrogen
    - D) Carbon

46. **Who was the first President of the United States?**
    - A) Thomas Jefferson
    - B) John Adams
    - C) George Washington
    - D) James Madison

47. **Which organ is responsible for pumping blood?**
    - A) Liver
    - B) Brain
    - C) Heart
    - D) Lungs

48. **What is the chemical symbol for water?**
    - A) H2O
    - B) CO2
    - C) O2
    - D) NaCl

49. **What is the largest land animal?**
    - A) Rhinoceros
    - B) Elephant
    - C) Hippopotamus
    - D) Giraffe

50. **Which is the smallest US state by area?**
    - A) Delaware
    - B) Rhode Island
    - C) Connecticut
    - D) Hawaii

51. **Who was the first man to walk on the moon?**
    - A) Buzz Aldrin
    - B) Yuri Gagarin
    - C) Neil Armstrong
    - D) Michael Collins

52. **What is the capital of France?**
    - A) Lyon
    - B) Marseille
    - C) Paris

- D) Bordeaux

53. **What is the primary function of the large intestine?**
    - A) Absorb nutrients
    - B) Produce bile
    - C) Absorb water
    - D) Filter blood

54. **Which planet is known for its rings?**
    - A) Neptune
    - B) Uranus
    - C) Jupiter
    - D) Saturn

55. **What is the smallest particle of an element?**
    - A) Molecule
    - B) Atom
    - C) Proton
    - D) Neutron

56. **Which country is the Eiffel Tower located in?**
    - A) Italy
    - B) Germany
    - C) Spain
    - D) France

57. **Who is the author of "To Kill a Mockingbird"?**
    - A) Harper Lee
    - B) J.D. Salinger
    - C) F. Scott Fitzgerald
    - D) Truman Capote

58. **What is the chemical symbol for table salt?**
    - A) NaCl
    - B) KCl

- C) MgCl2
- D) CaCl2

59. **What is the most populous country in the world?**
    - A) India
    - B) United States
    - C) China
    - D) Indonesia

60. **Which ocean is the Bermuda Triangle located in?**
    - A) Arctic Ocean
    - B) Atlantic Ocean
    - C) Indian Ocean
    - D) Pacific Ocean

61. **Who painted "The Last Supper"?**
    - A) Raphael
    - B) Leonardo da Vinci
    - C) Michelangelo
    - D) Titian

62. **What is the capital of Germany?**
    - A) Munich
    - B) Berlin
    - C) Frankfurt
    - D) Hamburg

63. **What is the main ingredient in chocolate?**
    - A) Vanilla
    - B) Cocoa
    - C) Sugar
    - D) Milk

64. **Who was the famous civil rights leader who delivered the "I Have a Dream" speech?**

  - A) Malcolm X
  - B) Martin Luther King Jr.
  - C) Rosa Parks
  - D) Nelson Mandela

65. **What is 12 squared?**
  - A) 124
  - B) 144
  - C) 164
  - D) 184

66. **Which animal is known as the King of the Jungle?**
  - A) Elephant
  - B) Tiger
  - C) Lion
  - D) Bear

67. **What is the main currency used in Japan?**
  - A) Yen
  - B) Won
  - C) Dollar
  - D) Euro

68. **Who was the Greek goddess of wisdom?**
  - A) Hera
  - B) Athena
  - C) Aphrodite
  - D) Artemis

69. **What is the largest desert in the world?**
  - A) Gobi
  - B) Sahara
  - C) Arabian
  - D) Kalahari

70. **Who wrote the novel "Moby-Dick"?**
    - A) Herman Melville
    - B) Nathaniel Hawthorne
    - C) Edgar Allan Poe
    - D) Mark Twain

71. **What is the name of the galaxy that contains our Solar System?**
    - A) Andromeda Galaxy
    - B) Milky Way Galaxy
    - C) Whirlpool Galaxy
    - D) Sombrero Galaxy

72. **Which vitamin is produced when a person is exposed to sunlight?**
    - A) Vitamin A
    - B) Vitamin B
    - C) Vitamin C
    - D) Vitamin D

73. **What is the capital of Russia?**
    - A) St. Petersburg
    - B) Moscow
    - C) Novosibirsk
    - D) Kazan

74. **What is the smallest bone in the human body?**
    - A) Femur
    - B) Stapes
    - C) Tibia
    - D) Ulna

75. **Who discovered the law of gravity?**
    - A) Albert Einstein
    - B) Isaac Newton
    - C) Galileo Galilei
    - D) Johannes Kepler

76. **What is the largest organ in the human body?**
   - A) Heart
   - B) Liver
   - C) Skin
   - D) Brain

77. **What is the main ingredient in sushi?**
   - A) Rice
   - B) Bread
   - C) Pasta
   - D) Potato

78. **Which planet is known as the Evening Star?**
   - A) Mars
   - B) Venus
   - C) Neptune
   - D) Mercury

79. **What is the approximate circumference of the Earth at the equator?**
   - A) 20,000 km
   - B) 30,000 km
   - C) 40,000 km
   - D) 50,000 km

80. **Who was the first woman to fly solo across the Atlantic Ocean?**
   - A) Bessie Coleman
   - B) Amelia Earhart
   - C) Harriet Quimby
   - D) Jacqueline Cochran

81. **What is the capital city of Spain?**
   - A) Barcelona
   - B) Madrid

- C) Valencia
- D) Seville

82. **What is the largest species of shark?**
    - A) Great White Shark
    - B) Tiger Shark
    - C) Whale Shark
    - D) Hammerhead Shark

83. **Which country is known for inventing the pizza?**
    - A) France
    - B) Italy
    - C) Greece
    - D) Spain

84. **What is the chemical symbol for iron?**
    - A) Ir
    - B) Fe
    - C) I
    - D) In

85. **Who wrote "The Catcher in the Rye"?**
    - A) J.D. Salinger
    - B) F. Scott Fitzgerald
    - C) John Steinbeck
    - D) Ernest Hemingway

86. **Which organ is responsible for detoxifying chemicals in the body?**
    - A) Heart
    - B) Liver
    - C) Lungs
    - D) Kidneys

87. **What is the largest island in the world?**
    - A) Madagascar

- B) Borneo
- C) Greenland
- D) New Guinea

88. **Which is the smallest planet in our Solar System?**
    - A) Mars
    - B) Venus
    - C) Mercury
    - D) Earth

89. **What is the capital of Mexico?**
    - A) Guadalajara
    - B) Monterrey
    - C) Cancún
    - D) Mexico City

90. **Who is the author of the "Harry Potter" series?**
    - A) J.R.R. Tolkien
    - B) C.S. Lewis
    - C) J.K. Rowling
    - D) Suzanne Collins

91. **What is the chemical symbol for silver?**
    - A) Au
    - B) Ag
    - C) Pb
    - D) Pt

92. **What is the most spoken language in the world?**
    - A) English
    - B) Spanish
    - C) Mandarin
    - D) Hindi

93. **What is the largest type of whale?**

- A) Humpback Whale
- B) Blue Whale
- C) Sperm Whale
- D) Gray Whale

94. **Which country is known for the Eiffel Tower?**
    - A) Italy
    - B) Germany
    - C) France
    - D) Spain

95. **Which planet is known as the Morning Star?**
    - A) Venus
    - B) Mars
    - C) Mercury
    - D) Jupiter

96. **Which element is essential for bones and teeth?**
    - A) Iron
    - B) Calcium
    - C) Potassium
    - D) Sodium

97. **Who invented the light bulb?**
    - A) Nikola Tesla
    - B) Thomas Edison
    - C) Benjamin Franklin
    - D) Alexander Graham Bell

98. **What is the most abundant mineral in the human body?**
    - A) Iron
    - B) Calcium
    - C) Magnesium
    - D) Zinc

99. **What is the capital of India?**
  - A) Mumbai
  - B) New Delhi
  - C) Kolkata
  - D) Bangalore

100. **Who was the first person to reach the South Pole?**
  - A) Ernest Shackleton
  - B) Robert Falcon Scott
  - C) Roald Amundsen
  - D) Edmund Hillary

101. **What is the largest species of bear?**
  - A) Grizzly Bear
  - B) Polar Bear
  - C) Black Bear
  - D) Panda Bear

102. **Which planet is known for its Great Red Spot?**
  - A) Mars
  - B) Jupiter
  - C) Saturn
  - D) Neptune

103. **What is the capital of Greece?**
  - A) Athens
  - B) Sparta
  - C) Thessaloniki
  - D) Corinth

104. **What is the main ingredient in hummus?**
  - A) Lentils
  - B) Chickpeas
  - C) Black Beans
  - D) Soybeans

105. **Which continent is the Sahara Desert located on?**
   - A) Asia
   - B) Africa
   - C) Australia
   - D) South America

106. **What is the most abundant element in the universe?**
   - A) Helium
   - B) Oxygen
   - C) Carbon
   - D) Hydrogen

107. **Who painted the "Sistine Chapel Ceiling"?**
   - A) Leonardo da Vinci
   - B) Raphael
   - C) Michelangelo
   - D) Caravaggio

108. **What is the capital of Japan?**
   - A) Osaka
   - B) Kyoto
   - C) Tokyo
   - D) Hiroshima

109. **What is the smallest unit of life?**
   - A) Tissue
   - B) Organ
   - C) Cell
   - D) Molecule

110. **Who is known as the Bard of Avon?**
   - A) Geoffrey Chaucer
   - B) William Wordsworth
   - C) William Shakespeare

- D) John Milton

111. **What is the hottest planet in our Solar System?**
   - A) Mercury
   - B) Venus
   - C) Mars
   - D) Jupiter

112. **Who discovered America in 1492?**
   - A) Ferdinand Magellan
   - B) Christopher Columbus
   - C) Vasco da Gama
   - D) Leif Erikson

113. **What is the chemical symbol for potassium?**
   - A) P
   - B) Po
   - C) K
   - D) Pt

114. **Which planet is known as the Earth's twin?**
   - A) Mars
   - B) Venus
   - C) Mercury
   - D) Jupiter

115. **What is the hardest known natural material?**
   - A) Steel
   - B) Diamond
   - C) Quartz
   - D) Graphite

116. **What is the capital of South Africa?**
   - A) Johannesburg
   - B) Cape Town

- C) Pretoria
- D) Durban

117. **Who wrote "Les Misérables"?**
    - A) Victor Hugo
    - B) Charles Dickens
    - C) Leo Tolstoy
    - D) Alexandre Dumas

118. **What is the chemical symbol for lead?**
    - A) Pb
    - B) Ld
    - C) Sn
    - D) Hg

119. **Which is the most populous city in the world?**
    - A) Tokyo
    - B) New York
    - C) Shanghai
    - D) Mumbai

120. **What is the main ingredient in bread?**
    - A) Rice
    - B) Wheat
    - C) Corn
    - D) Oats

121. **Who was the first President of the United States?**
    - A) John Adams
    - B) Thomas Jefferson
    - C) George Washington
    - D) James Madison

122. **What is the largest lake in the world by area?**
    - A) Lake Superior

  - B) Caspian Sea
  - C) Lake Victoria
  - D) Lake Michigan

123. **What is the most abundant gas in the Earth's atmosphere?**
  - A) Oxygen
  - B) Argon
  - C) Nitrogen
  - D) Carbon Dioxide

124. **Who wrote "The Divine Comedy"?**
  - A) Dante Alighieri
  - B) Geoffrey Chaucer
  - C) John Milton
  - D) Homer

125. **What is the speed of light in a vacuum?**
  - A) 300,000 km/s
  - B) 150,000 km/s
  - C) 450,000 km/s
  - D) 600,000 km/s

126. **Which planet is known for its rings?**
  - A) Jupiter
  - B) Uranus
  - C) Saturn
  - D) Neptune

127. **What is the capital of Argentina?**
  - A) Buenos Aires
  - B) Córdoba
  - C) Rosario
  - D) Mendoza

128. **Who wrote "The Iliad"?**

- A) Virgil
- B) Homer
- C) Ovid
- D) Sophocles

129. **What is the largest type of penguin?**
   - A) Emperor Penguin
   - B) King Penguin
   - C) Adelie Penguin
   - D) Gentoo Penguin

130. **What is the most common blood type?**
   - A) A
   - B) B
   - C) AB
   - D) O

131. **Which element is known as the building block of life?**
   - A) Carbon
   - B) Hydrogen
   - C) Oxygen
   - D) Nitrogen

132. **Who painted "Guernica"?**
   - A) Salvador Dalí
   - B) Pablo Picasso
   - C) Francisco Goya
   - D) Joan Miró

133. **What is the largest species of lizard?**
   - A) Komodo Dragon
   - B) Iguana
   - C) Monitor Lizard
   - D) Gecko

134. **Who was the first woman to win a Nobel Prize?**
    - A) Marie Curie
    - B) Rosalind Franklin
    - C) Ada Lovelace
    - D) Lise Meitner

135. **Which planet has the shortest day?**
    - A) Venus
    - B) Jupiter
    - C) Mars
    - D) Saturn

136. **What is the capital of Thailand?**
    - A) Chiang Mai
    - B) Phuket
    - C) Pattaya
    - D) Bangkok

137. **What is the most eaten food in the world?**
    - A) Bread
    - B) Rice
    - C) Pasta
    - D) Potatoes

138. **Which country has the most time zones?**
    - A) USA
    - B) Russia
    - C) China
    - D) Australia

139. **What is the main ingredient in tofu?**
    - A) Lentils
    - B) Chickpeas
    - C) Soybeans
    - D) Rice

140. **Who wrote "Anna Karenina"?**
   - A) Fyodor Dostoevsky
   - B) Leo Tolstoy
   - C) Anton Chekhov
   - D) Ivan Turgenev

141. **What is the capital of Brazil?**
   - A) São Paulo
   - B) Rio de Janeiro
   - C) Brasília
   - D) Salvador

142. **Who invented the World Wide Web?**
   - A) Bill Gates
   - B) Steve Jobs
   - C) Tim Berners-Lee
   - D) Larry Page

143. **What is the smallest country in the world?**
   - A) Monaco
   - B) Vatican City
   - C) San Marino
   - D) Liechtenstein

144. **Which gas is commonly known as laughing gas?**
   - A) Nitrogen
   - B) Oxygen
   - C) Nitrous Oxide
   - D) Carbon Dioxide

145. **Who wrote "The Hobbit"?**
   - A) J.R.R. Tolkien
   - B) C.S. Lewis
   - C) J.K. Rowling

- D) George R.R. Martin

146. **What is the largest type of deer?**
    - A) White-tailed Deer
    - B) Moose
    - C) Elk
    - D) Reindeer

147. **Which ocean is the largest by volume?**
    - A) Atlantic Ocean
    - B) Indian Ocean
    - C) Arctic Ocean
    - D) Pacific Ocean

148. **What is the hardest known metal?**
    - A) Iron
    - B) Tungsten
    - C) Titanium
    - D) Platinum

149. **Who composed the "Moonlight Sonata"?**
    - A) Wolfgang Amadeus Mozart
    - B) Johann Sebastian Bach
    - C) Ludwig van Beethoven
    - D) Franz Schubert

150. **Which element is known as the "King of Metals"?**
    - A) Gold
    - B) Silver
    - C) Platinum
    - D) Copper

QUESTIONS

** Answer True or False **

1.   The Earth's atmosphere is composed primarily of nitrogen and oxygen.

---

2.   The largest planet in our solar system is Jupiter.

---

3.   The Great Wall of China is visible from space with the naked eye.

---

4.   The human body contains more bacteria cells than human cells.

---

5.   The speed of light is approximately 299,792,458 meters per second.

---

6.   The Earth is perfectly round.

---

7.   The human brain contains about 86 billion neurons.

---

8.   The largest ocean on Earth is the Pacific Ocean.

---

9.   The Earth's magnetic field is constant and unchanging.

10. The sun is a star.

---

11. The human heart beats approximately 100,000 times a day.

---

12. The human body can survive for weeks without water.

---

13. The Earth's rotation is slowing down.

---

14. The universe is expanding.

---

15. The human body can only use 10% of its brain power.

---

16. The Earth's core is primarily composed of iron.

---

17. The human body can generate enough electricity to power a light bulb.

---

18. The human body can regenerate all its cells every seven years.

---

19. The human eye can see over 10 million different colors.

---

20. The human body is approximately 60% water.

---

21. The human brain is the only organ that can feel pain.

---

22. The human body can survive for a short period of time without oxygen.

---

23. The Earth's atmosphere protects us from harmful radiation from the sun.

---

24. The human body can only use one sense at a time.

---

25. The human body contains more than 600 muscles.

---

26. The first computer was invented in the 1940s.

---

27. The internet was originally developed for military purposes.

---

28. The first mobile phone was invented in the 1980s.

29. The first commercial website was launched in 1991.

30. The first email was sent in 1971.

31. The first computer virus was created in the 1990s.

32. The world's first artificial satellite, Sputnik 1, was launched in 1957.

33. The first personal computer was invented in the 1970s.

34. The first video game was created in the 1990s.

35. The first commercial smartphone was launched in 2007.

36. The first 3D printer was invented in the 1980s.

37. The first social media platform was created in the 1990s.

38. The first computer mouse was invented in 1964.

----

39. The first computer program was written in the 1970s.

----

40. The first digital camera was invented in the 1970s.

----

41. The first microprocessor was invented in the 1970s.

----

42. The first internet browser was created in the 1980s.

----

43. The first commercial laser printer was invented in the 1970s.

----

44. The first commercial GPS receiver was invented in the 1980s.

----

45. The human heart can beat outside the body.

----

46. The human body can regenerate some tissues.

----

47. The human body can only use one type of blood.

----

48. The human body can fight off infections with its own immune system.

49. The human body can produce its own vitamin D from sunlight.

50. The human body can only use one type of antibiotic.

51. Water consists of two hydrogen atoms and one oxygen atom.

52. All metals conduct electricity. (Some are insulators)

53. The sun is a yellow dwarf star.

54. The moon produces its own light. (It reflects sunlight)

55. Mercury is the only metal that is liquid at room temperature.

56. All planets revolve around the sun in the same direction.

57. Most sedimentary rocks consist of layers.

----

58. Earthquakes only occur in the oceans.

----

59. Lightning is an electrical discharge that occurs in the atmosphere.

----

60. All volcanoes erupt violently.

----

61. Winds are formed as a result of differences in atmospheric pressure.

----

62. Acid rain is caused only by volcanic eruptions.

----

63. Ozone protects the Earth from harmful ultraviolet radiation.

----

64. Clouds are made up only of water vapor.

----

65. The water cycle in nature is a continuous process.

----

66. All stars have the same size and mass.

----

67. Black holes have enormous gravity.

68. Stars produce their energy from cold nuclear reactions.

69. Galaxies are made up of billions of stars.

70. The universe is constant and unchanging.

71. Light has a finite speed.

72. Gravity is the only force acting on planets.

73. Tides are caused by the Moon's gravity.

74. All living things need oxygen to survive.

75. Photosynthesis is a process by which plants produce their own food.

76. All plants require the same amount of water and light.

77. Cells are the basic unit of life.

78. All viruses are harmful.

79. Genes carry genetic information.

80. Evolution is a rapid process.

81. Global warming causes the Earth to warm.

82. Air pollution does not affect human health.

83. Water pollution threatens aquatic life.

84. Excessive use of pesticides does not affect the environment.

85. Deforestation leads to the extinction of species.

86. All natural resources are renewable.

87. Renewable energy is environmentally friendly.

----

88. Organic farming does not produce sufficient crops.

----

89. Climate change threatens global food security.

----

90. Salt water is suitable for drinking directly.

----

91. Computers operate on a binary system.

----

92. Programming is an easy and simple process.

----

93. The Internet is a global network that connects computers.

----

94. All websites are secure.

----

95. Artificial intelligence is a rapidly developing field.

----

96. Robots can perform all human tasks.

----

97. Solar energy is a renewable energy source.

---

98. Nuclear energy is risk-free.

---

99. Electric cars are environmentally friendly.

---

100. All plastics are biodegradable.

---

101. 3D printing is an advanced technology.

---

102. All medicines are completely safe.

---

103. Vaccines protect against infectious diseases.

---

104. All antibiotics are effective against all types of bacteria.

---

105. Regular checkups are important for early detection of diseases.

---

106. Exercise does not affect mental health.

---

107. A healthy diet is important for overall health.

108. Sleep is not essential for health.

----

109. Smoking causes many diseases.

----

110. Coffee is always harmful.

----

111. Education is important for social and economic progress.

----

112. All cultures are the same.

----

113. Cultural diversity enriches societies.

----

114. Poverty does not affect health.

----

115. Social justice is important for building a cohesive society.

----

116. Wars do not affect the economy.

----

117. International cooperation is important for solving global problems.

----

118. Politics does not affect people's lives.

----

119. Human rights are universal.

----

120. Democracy is the only effective political system.

----

121. The sum of the angles of a triangle is 180 degrees.

----

122. All even numbers are divisible by 4.

----

123. Zero is neither a positive nor a negative number.

----

124. Decimals cannot be converted to fractions.

----

125. Pi is an important mathematical constant.

----

126. Gravity pulls objects toward the Earth.

----

127. Mass and weight are always equal.

128. Energy can neither be created nor destroyed.

----

129. Velocity and acceleration are always equal.

----

130. Rotational motion is motion around an axis.

----

131. Atoms are made up of protons, neutrons, and electrons.

----

132. All chemical reactions release heat.

----

133. Water is a chemical compound.

----

134. All chemical compounds are toxic.

----

135. The periodic table arranges the chemical elements.

----

136. Plant cells contain chloroplasts.

----

137. All animals have the same number of chromosomes.

138. Reproduction is the production of new individuals.

139. All living things reproduce in the same way.

140. Heredity is the transmission of traits from parents to offspring.

141. All planets have moons.

142. Meteors are meteors that burn up in the atmosphere.

143. All stars are close to Earth at the same distance.

144. Earth is a rocky planet.

145. Arabic is a rich language.

146. All languages are similar in their structure.

147. Reading is important to expand knowledge.

148. Writing is not important.

149. Communication is important in life.

150. Elephants are the only animals that can't jump